T0061476

The Complete
Keyboard Player
Great Standards

Published by
Wise Publications
14-15 Berners Street,
London W1T 3LJ, UK.

Exclusive Distributors:
Music Sales Limited
Distribution Centre, Newmarket Road,
Bury St Edmunds, Suffolk IP33 3YB, UK.
Music Sales Pty Limited
Units 3-4, 17 Willfox Street, Condell Park
NSW 2200, Australia.

Order No. AM1009569
ISBN 978-1-78305-732-0

This book © Copyright 2014 Wise Publications,
a division of Music Sales Limited.

Unauthorised reproduction of any part of this
publication by any means including photocopying is an
infringement of copyright.

Edited by Jenni Norey.
Music processed by Paul Ewers Music Design.

Printed in the EU.

Your Guarantee of Quality
As publishers, we strive to produce every book to the
highest commercial standards.
This book has been carefully designed to minimise awkward
page turns and to make playing from it a real pleasure.
Particular care has been given to specifying acid-free, neutral-sized paper
made from pulps which have not been elemental chlorine bleached.
This pulp is from farmed sustainable forests and was
produced with special regard for the environment.
Throughout, the printing and binding have been planned to
ensure a sturdy, attractive publication which should give years of enjoyment.
If your copy fails to meet our high standards,
please inform us and we will gladly replace it.

www.musicsales.com

The Complete
Keyboard Player
Great Standards

Wise Publications
part of The Music Sales Group
London/New York/Paris/Sydney/Copenhagen/Berlin/Madrid/Hong Kong/Tokyo

Contents

Master Chord Chart

C
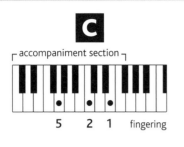
accompaniment section
5 2 1 fingering

Cm
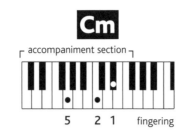
accompaniment section
5 2 1 fingering

C 7
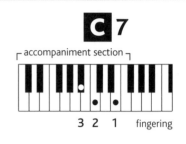
accompaniment section
3 2 1 fingering

D♭(C♯)
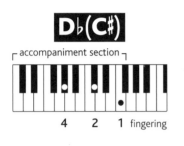
accompaniment section
4 2 1 fingering

D♭(C♯)m
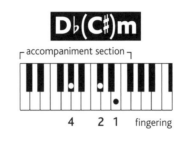
accompaniment section
4 2 1 fingering

D♭(C♯) 7
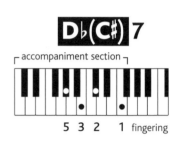
accompaniment section
5 3 2 1 fingering

D
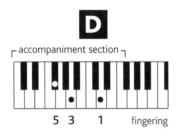
accompaniment section
5 3 1 fingering

Dm
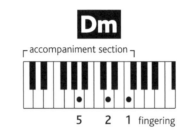
accompaniment section
5 2 1 fingering

D 7
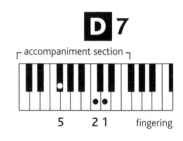
accompaniment section
5 2 1 fingering

E♭(D♯)
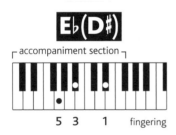
accompaniment section
5 3 1 fingering

E♭(D♯)m
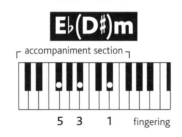
accompaniment section
5 3 1 fingering

E♭(D♯) 7
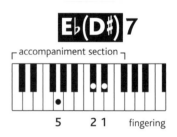
accompaniment section
5 2 1 fingering

E
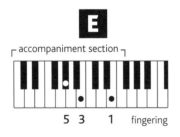
accompaniment section
5 3 1 fingering

Em
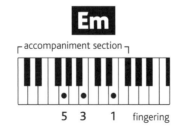
accompaniment section
5 3 1 fingering

E 7
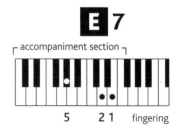
accompaniment section
5 2 1 fingering

F
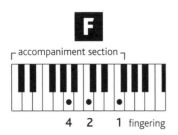
accompaniment section
4 2 1 fingering

Fm
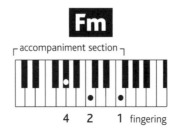
accompaniment section
4 2 1 fingering

F 7
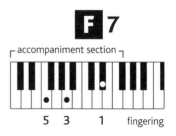
accompaniment section
5 3 1 fingering

Master Chord Chart

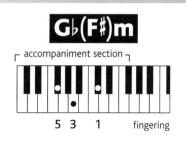

G♭(F#)

accompaniment section

5 3 1   fingering

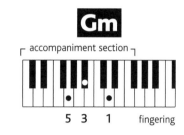

G♭(F#)m

accompaniment section

5 3 1   fingering

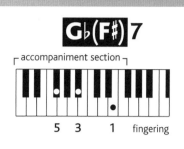

G♭(F#)7

accompaniment section

5 3 1   fingering

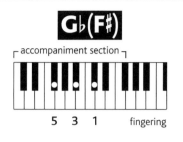

G

accompaniment section

5 3 1   fingering

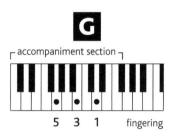

Gm

accompaniment section

5 3 1   fingering

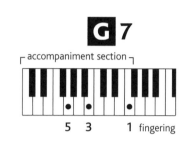

G7

accompaniment section

5 3 1 fingering

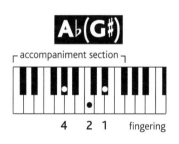

A♭(G#)

accompaniment section

4 2 1   fingering

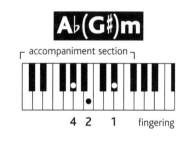

A♭(G#)m

accompaniment section

4 2 1   fingering

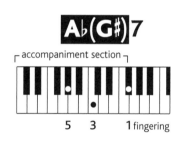

A♭(G#)7

accompaniment section

5 3 1 fingering

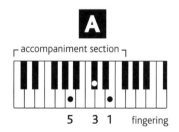

A

accompaniment section

5 3 1   fingering

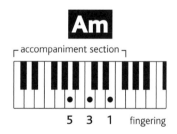

Am

accompaniment section

5 3 1   fingering

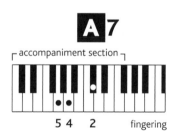

A7

accompaniment section

5 4 2   fingering

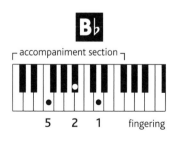

B♭

accompaniment section

5 2 1   fingering

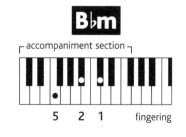

B♭m

accompaniment section

5 2 1   fingering

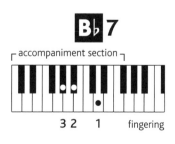

B♭7

accompaniment section

3 2 1   fingering

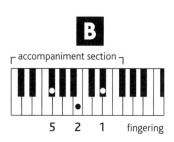

B

accompaniment section

5 2 1   fingering

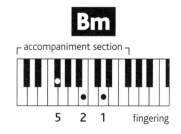

Bm

accompaniment section

5 2 1   fingering

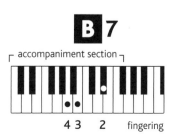

B7

accompaniment section

4 3 2   fingering

Almost Like Being In Love

Words by Alan Jay Lerner
Music by Frederick Loewe

Voice: **Harp**
Rhythm: **Foxtrot**
Tempo: ♩ = 125

What a day this has been! What a rare mood I'm in! Why, it's

al - most like be - ing in love._____ There's a

smile on my face for the whole hu - man race. Why, it's

al - most like be - ing in love!_____ All the

© Copyright 1947 The Lerner Heirs Publishing Designee and The Loewe Foundation Publishing Designee.
EMI U Catalog Inc.
All Rights Reserved. International Copyright Secured.

mu - sic of life seems to be,_____ like a

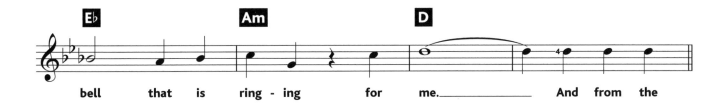

bell that is ring - ing for me._____ And from the

way that I feel when that bell starts to peal I would

swear I was fall - ing, I could swear I was fall - ing, it's

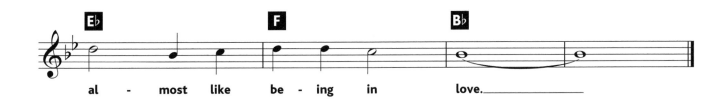

al - most like be - ing in love._____

Blue Moon

Words by Lorenz Hart
Music by Richard Rodgers

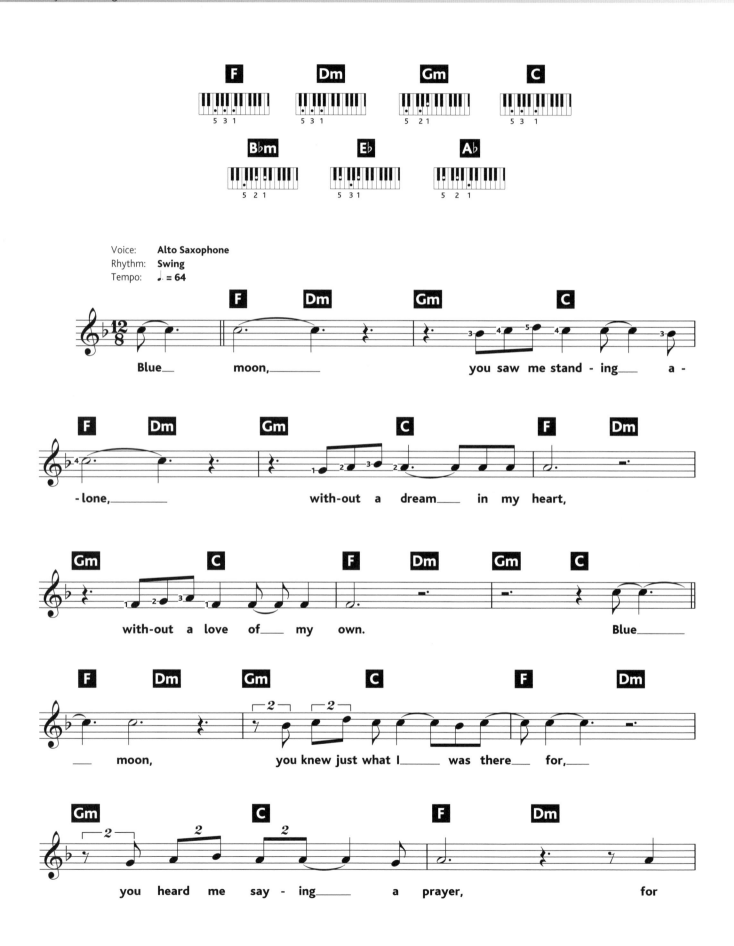

© Copyright 1934 EMI-Robbins Catalog Inc.
EMI United Partnership Limited.
All Rights Reserved. International Copyright Secured.

A Certain Smile

Words by Paul Francis Webster
Music by Sammy Fain

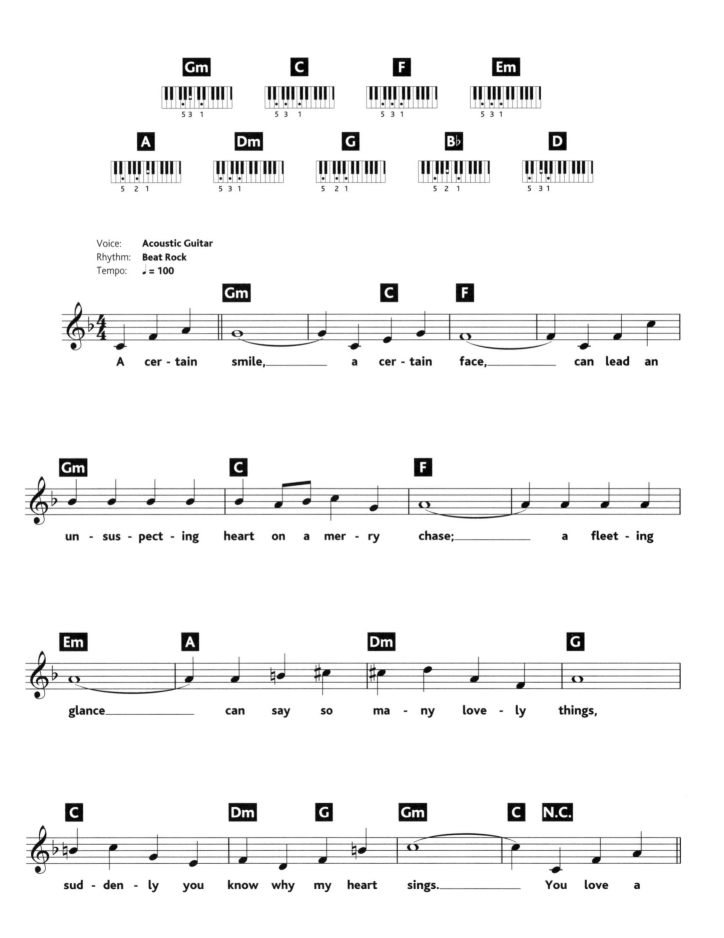

© Copyright 1958 EMI Robbins Catalog Inc.
EMI United Partnership Limited.
All Rights Reserved. International Copyright Secured.

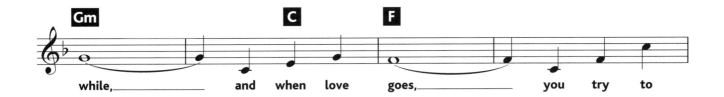

while,_____ and when love goes,_____ you try to

hide the tears in - side with a cheer - ful pose;_____ but in the

hush of night ex - act - ly like a bit - ter - sweet re -

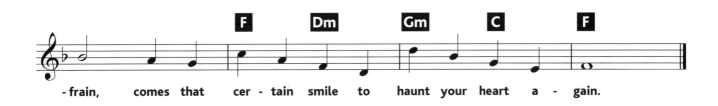

- frain, comes that cer - tain smile to haunt your heart a - gain.

East Of The Sun (And West Of The Moon)

Words & Music by Brooks Bowman

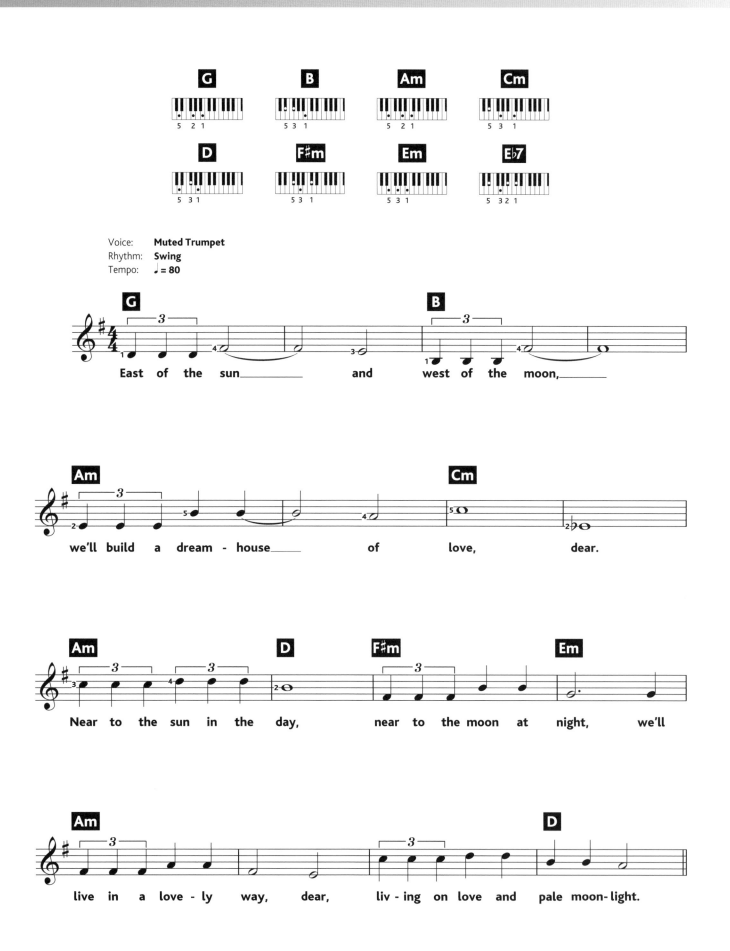

© Copyright 1934 Princetown University Triangle Club/Santly Brothers Incorporated, USA.
Campbell Connelly & Company Limited.
All Rights Reserved. International Copyright Secured.

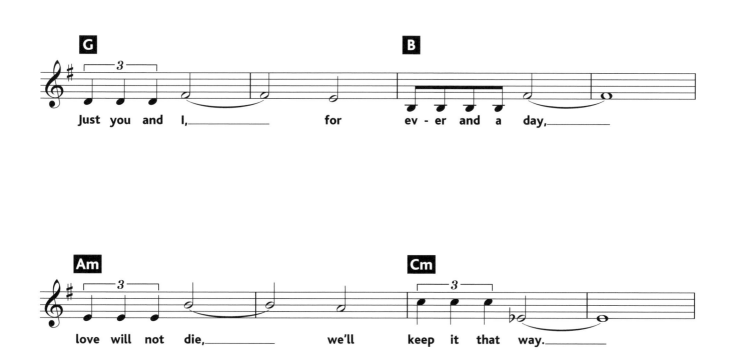

Just you and I,_____ for ev - er and a day,_____

love will not die,_____ we'll keep it that way._____

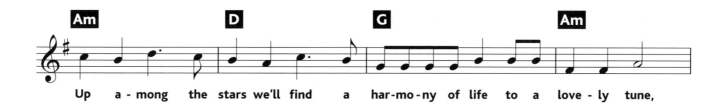

Up a - mong the stars we'll find a har-mo-ny of life to a love - ly tune,

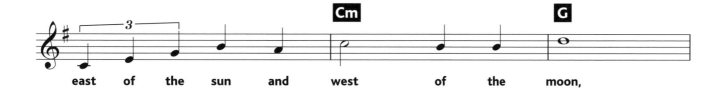

east of the sun and west of the moon,

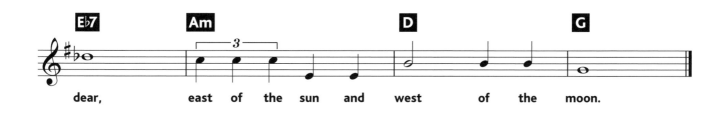

dear, east of the sun and west of the moon.

Georgia On My Mind

Words by Stuart Gorrell
Music by Hoagy Carmichael

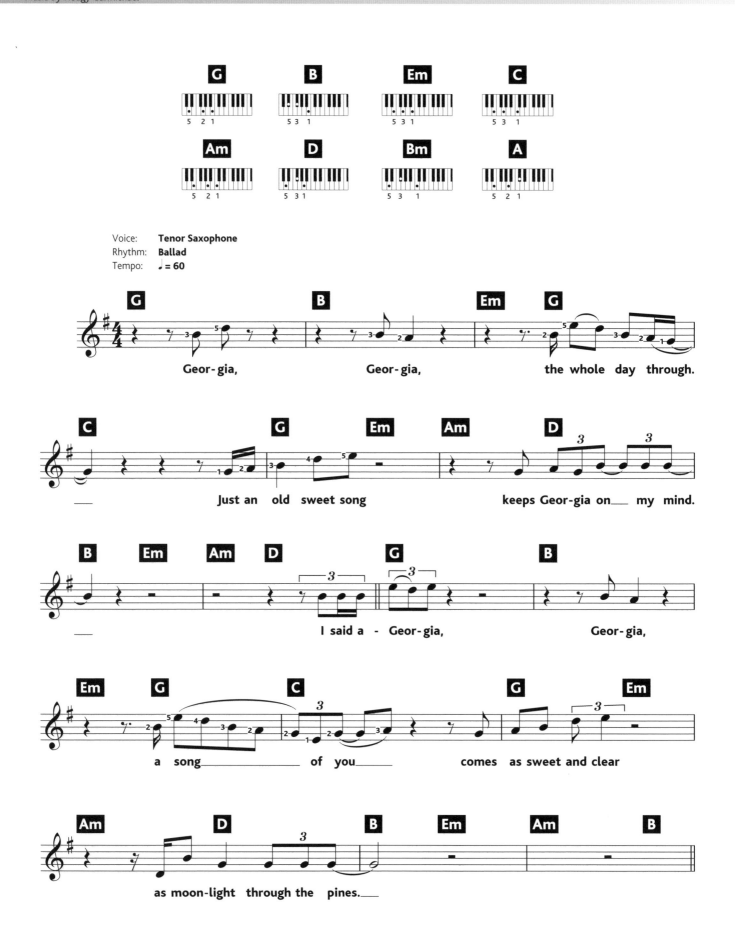

Voice: **Tenor Saxophone**
Rhythm: **Ballad**
Tempo: ♩ = 60

Geor-gia, Geor-gia, the whole day through.

— Just an old sweet song keeps Geor-gia on___ my mind.

— I said a - Geor-gia, Geor-gia,

a song_____ of you___ comes as sweet and clear

as moon-light through the pines.___

© Copyright 1930, Renewed 1957 Southern Music Publishing Company Incorporated, USA
Administered by Campbell Connelly & Company Limited for UK, Eire, Belgium, France, Holland, Switzerland, Fiji, Gibraltar,
Hong Kong, Malaysia, Saint Helena, Sierra Leone, Singapore and Sri Lanka.
All Rights Reserved. International Copyright Secured.

Oth-er arms   reach___ out   to   me,___   oth-er eyes   smile___

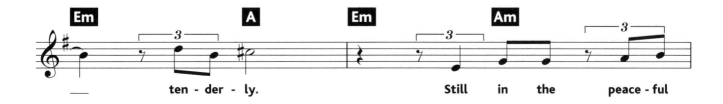

___   ten - der - ly.   Still   in   the   peace - ful

dreams I   see___   the road   leads back   to   you.___   I said

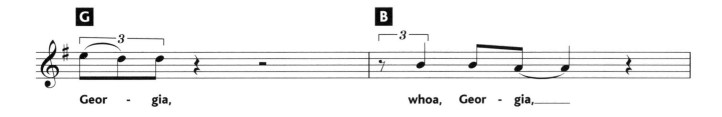

Geor - gia,   whoa,   Geor - gia,___

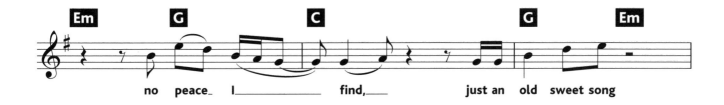

no   peace_   I___   find,___   just an   old   sweet song

keeps Geor-gia___   on   my   mind.___

Goodnight Sweetheart

Words & Music by Ray Noble, Jimmy Campbell & Reg Connelly

Voice: **Alto Saxophone**
Rhythm: **Slow swing**
Tempo: ♩ = 100

Good - night, sweet-heart, all my pray'rs are for you,

good - night sweet - heart, I'll be watch - ing o'er you,

tears and part - ing may make us for - lorn

but with the dawn, a new day is born. So I'll say

© Copyright 1931 Campbell Connelly & Co. Limited and Redwood Music Limited (1963) for accepted British Reversionary Territories
(Inc. UK, Canada, Australia, South Africa) and Spain.
© Copyright 1931 Campbell Connelly & Co. Limited for the rest of the World.
All Rights Reserved. International Copyright Secured.

Good - night, sweet - heart, sleep will ban - ish sor - row,

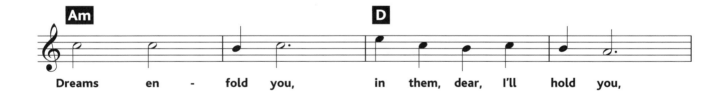

good - night, sweet - heart, till we meet to - mor - row.

Dreams en - fold you, in them, dear, I'll hold you,

good - night, sweet - heart, good - night.

I'm Beginning To See The Light

Words & Music by Duke Ellington, Harry James, Johnny Hodges & Don George

Voice: **Piano**
Rhythm: **Swing**
Tempo: ♩ = 125

I nev - er cared much for moon - lit skies, I

nev - er winked back at fire - flies, but now that the stars are

in your eyes, I'm be - gin - ning to see the light. I

nev - er went in for aft - er - glow, or can - dle - light on the

mis - tle - toe, but now when you turn the lamp down low, I'm be -

© Copyright 1944 Alamo Music Incorporated.
Chester Music Limited trading as Campbell Connelly & Co. for British Commonwealth (excluding Australia/Canada/New Zealand)
and Europe/Redwood Music Limited for British Commonwealth, Ireland and Spain.
All Rights Reserved. International Copyright Secured.

Lara's Theme (Somewhere My Love)

Words by Paul Francis Webster
Music by Maurice Jarre

© Copyright 1965 & 1966 Webster Music Company/EMI Robbins Catalogue Incorporated.
EMI United Partnership Limited/Rondor Music International.
All Rights Reserved. International Copyright Secured.

Some - day_____ we'll meet a - gain my love,_____

some - day_____ when - ev - er the spring breaks through._____

You'll come to me_____ out of the long a - go,_____

warm as the wind_____ soft as the kiss of snow._____

Till then my sweet_____ think of me now and then._____

God - speed, my love,_____ till you are mine a - gain._____

Moonlight Serenade

Words by Mitchell Parish
Music by Glenn Miller

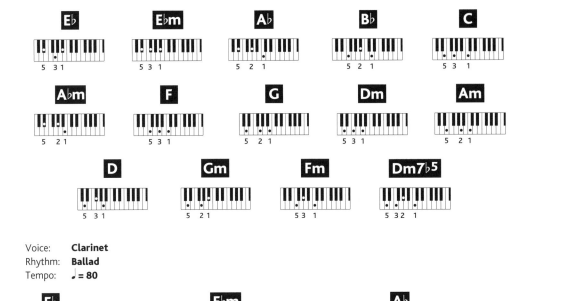

Voice: **Clarinet**
Rhythm: **Ballad**
Tempo: ♩ = **80**

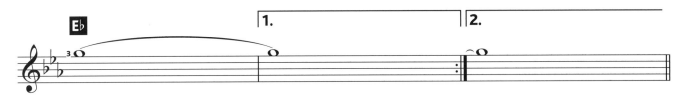

© Copyright 1939 EMI-Robbins Catalog Inc.
EMI United Partnership Limited.
All Rights Reserved. International Copyright Secured.

Over The Rainbow

Words by E.Y. Harburg
Music by Harold Arlen

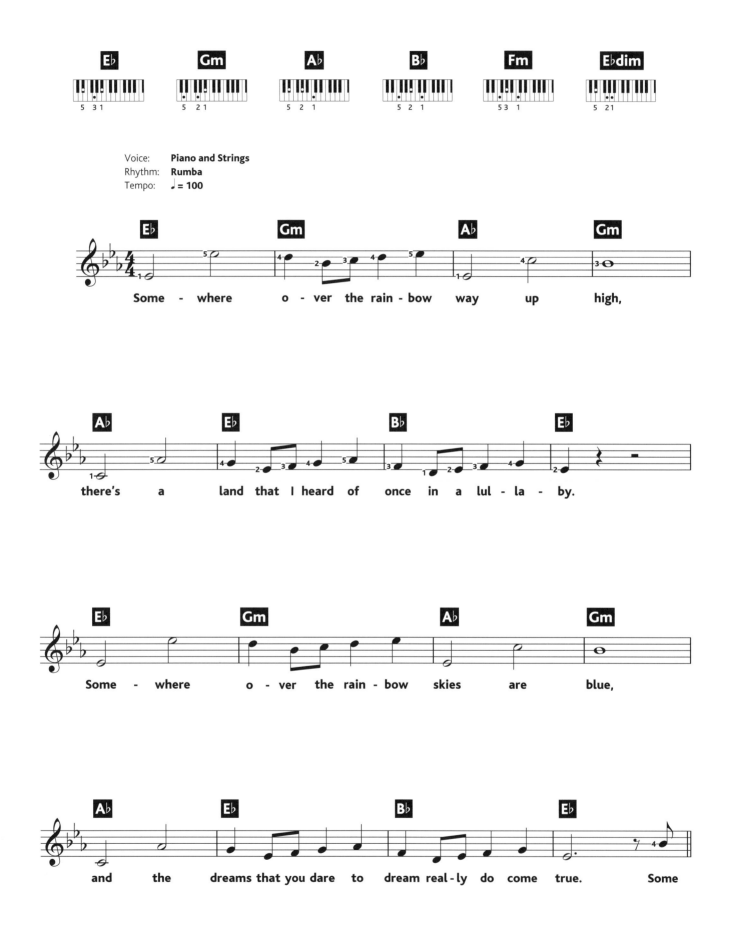

© Copyright 1938 EMI Feist Catalog Incorporated.
EMI United Partnership Limited.
All Rights Reserved. International Copyright Secured.

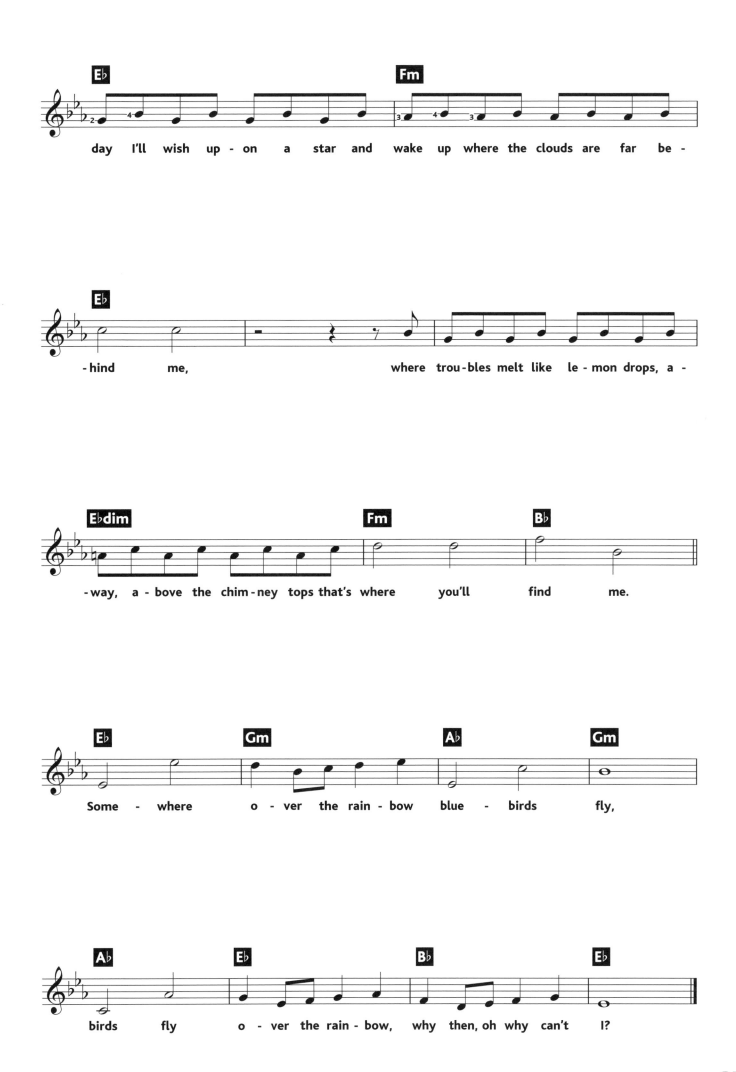

Pennies From Heaven

Words by Johnny Burke
Music by Arthur Johnston

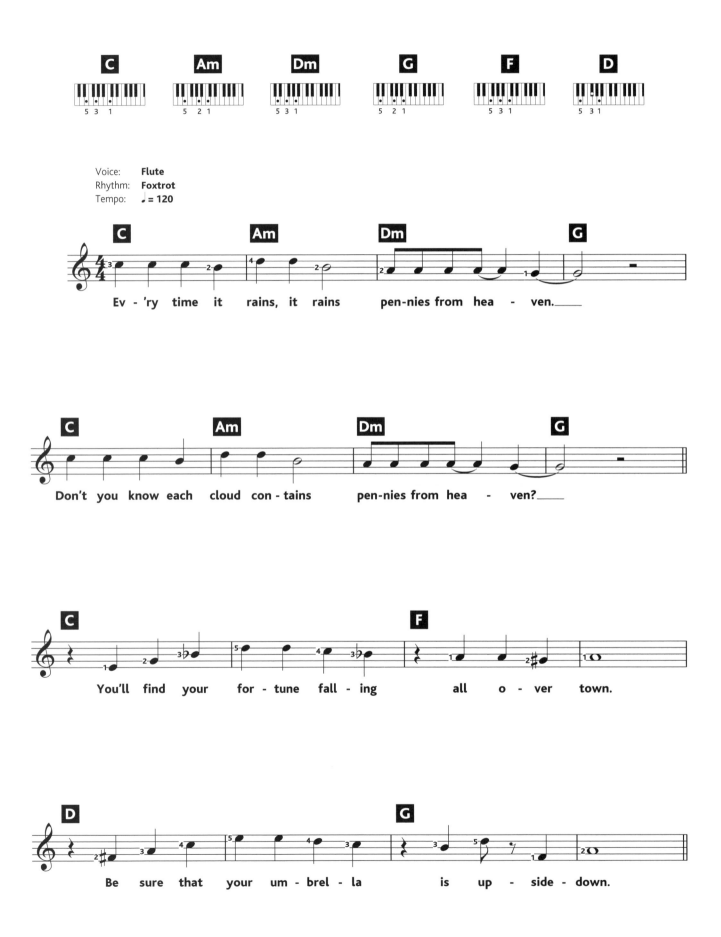

© Copyright 1936 Santly-Joy Inc.
Administered by Campbell Connelly & Company Limited for the British Commonwealth excluding Australasia and Canada.
All Rights Reserved. International Copyright Secured.

Trade them for a pack - age of sun-shine and flow - ers._____

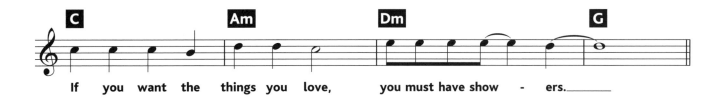

If you want the things you love, you must have show - ers._____

So when you hear it thund - er, don't run un - der a tree,_____ there'll be

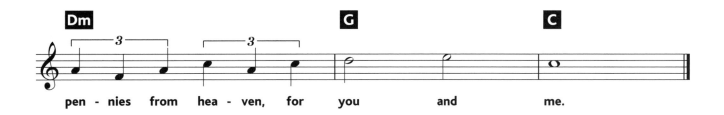

pen - nies from hea - ven, for you and me.

The Shadow Of Your Smile

Words by Paul Francis Webster
Music by Johnny Mandel

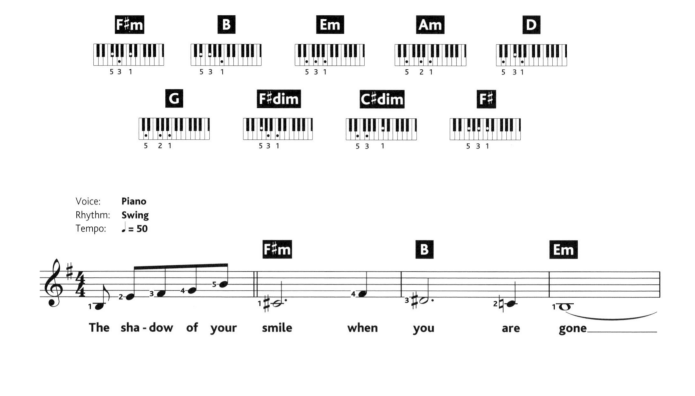

Voice: **Piano**
Rhythm: **Swing**
Tempo: ♩ = 50

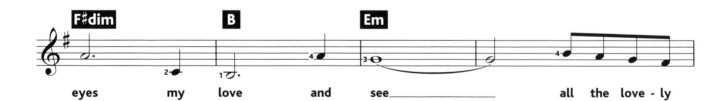

The sha-dow of your smile when you are gone_____

___ will col-our all my dreams and light the dawn._____ Look in-to my

eyes my love and see_____ all the love-ly

things you are to me._____ Our wist-ful lit-tle

© Copyright 1965 & 1967 EMI Miller Catalog Inc.
EMI United Partnership Limited.
All Rights Reserved. International Copyright Secured.

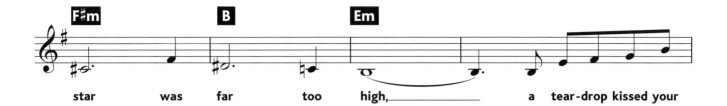

star   was   far   too   high,_____ a   tear-drop kissed your

lips   and   so   did   I._____   Now when I   re -

-mem - ber spring_____   all the joy that love can bring,_____ I will be re -

-mem - ber - ing_____   the sha-dow of your   smile._____

Singin' In The Rain

Words by Arthur Freed
Music by Nacio Herb Brown

© Copyright 1929 EMI Robbins Catalog Inc.
EMI United Partnership Limited.
All Rights Reserved. International Copyright Secured.

Tulips From Amsterdam

Words by Neumann & Bader
Music by Ralf Arnie

Voice: **Accordion**
Rhythm: **Waltz**
Tempo: ♩ = 160

When it's spring a - gain I'll bring a - gain

tu - lips from Am - ster - dam_____ with a

heart that's true I'll give to you

tu - lips from Am - ster - dam._____ I can't

© Copyright 1956 Beboton-Verlag GmbH, Germany.
Campbell Connelly & Company Limited.
All Rights Reserved. International Copyright Secured.

wait   un - til   the   day   you   fill

B♭

these   emp - ty   arms   of   mine_____ like   the

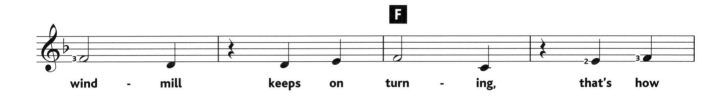

F

wind - mill   keeps   on   turn - ing,   that's   how

C   **F**

my   heart   keeps   on   yearn - ing   for   the

B♭   **F**

day   I   know   we   can_____ share   these

Gm   **C**   **F**

tu - lips   from   Am - ster - dam.

Under Paris Skies

Words by Jean Dréjac
Music by Hubert Giraud

© Copyright 1951 Editions Choudens, France.
Rights transferred to Premiere Music Group.
All Rights Reserved. International Copyright Secured.

- sire._____ Par - i - sian love can

bloom high in a sky - light room, or in a

gay ca - fé where hun - dreds of peo - ple can see._____

_____ Just look and see what hap-pened to me un - der

Par - is skies._____ Watch what you do, the

same thing can hap - pen to you._____

Where Do You Go To (My Lovely)

Words & Music by Peter Sarstedt

Voice: **Acoustic Guitar**
Rhythm: **Waltz**
Tempo: ♩ = **160**

You talk like Mar - len - e Diet - rich and you

dance like Zi Zi Jean Maire. Your

clothes are all made by Bal - main and there's dia - monds and

pearls in your hair, yes there are. You

live in a fan - cy a - part - ment, off the

© Copyright 1969 EMI United Partnership Limited.
All Rights Reserved. International Copyright Secured.

Bringing you the words and the music

All the latest music in print... rock & pop plus jazz, blues, country, classical and the best in West End show scores.

- Books to match your favourite CDs.

- Book-and-CD titles with high quality backing tracks for you to play along to. Now you can play guitar or piano with your favourite artist... or simply sing along!

- Audition songbooks with CD backing tracks for both male and female singers for all those with stars in their eyes.

- Can't read music? No problem, you can still play all the hits with our wide range of chord songbooks.

- Check out our range of instrumental tutorial titles, taking you from novice to expert in no time at all!

- Musical show scores include *The Phantom Of The Opera*, *Les Misérables*, *Mamma Mia* and many more hit productions.

- DVD master classes featuring the techniques of top artists.

Visit your local music shop or, in case of difficulty, contact the Marketing Department, Music Sales Limited, Newmarket Road, Bury St Edmunds, Suffolk, IP33 3YB, UK
marketing@musicsales.co.uk